Deep in the Desert

ISBN 979-8-218-06152-4

Deep

in

the

Desert

text by Karen McCarthy Eger
illustrations by Marie Lejeune

Deep in the desert where the cactus grow,

stars twinkle brightly, the sky's all aglow.

Watch a small mouse scurry,

He's always in a hurry.

Deep in the desert where the cactus grow.

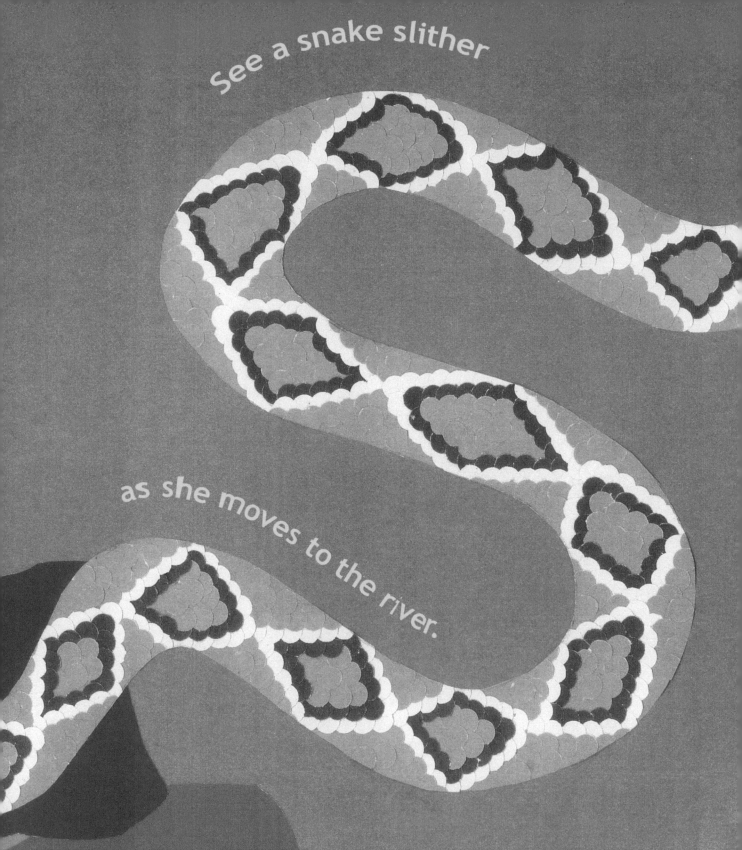

See a snake slither

as she moves to the river.

Deep in the desert where the cactus grow.

Gray coyote on the prowl,

lifts his muzzle, sniffs, and HOWLS...

Deep in the desert where the cactus grow.

Hear an owl hoot, wind whistles 'round the butte.

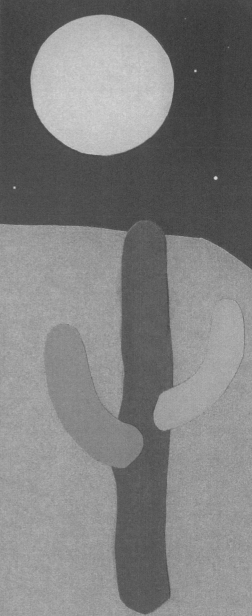

Deep in the desert where the cactus grow.

Feel

the earth

cool...

Moonlight puddles in a pool.

Deep in the desert where the cactus grow.

Now it's quiet   in the desert

where the cactus grow.

It's peaceful in the desert where the cactus grow.

It's nighttime in the desert where the cactus grow.

One square mile of living desert is worth a hundred great books and one brave deed is worth a thousand.

Edward Abbey

Planet Earth

Deserts

Deserts are parts of the Earth that are very dry.

Water might be underground, or might fall as rain and snow, but very little of it compared to other places.

Rivers and lakes might form after a big rain but dry up within hours or even minutes.

Deserts can be cold or hot, high or low, but they are always dry.

The animals and plants that live in them, including people, find special ways to get water.

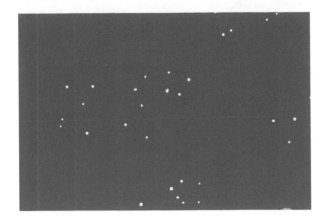

The Night Sky

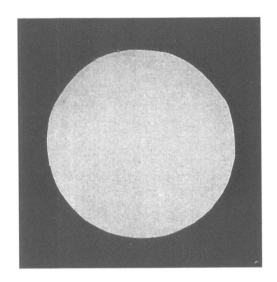

The Moon

A Butte

The night sky is full of points of light; stars, planets, and human-made satellites. The universe has more than 1,000,000,000,000,000,000,000,000 (200 billion trillion) stars. We don't see that many because they are far away and people light up the dark at night, causing light pollution in the sky. In places far from people, towns, and cities, billions more stars can be seen.

The moon is a round, dusty rock, smaller than Earth. There is water on it, trapped in tiny glass beads, in craters, and maybe more places. The light we see from the moon is a reflection of the sun, as if the moon is a mirror for the sun's light.

A butte (rhymes with "cute") is a rock hill with steep sides and a flat top standing by itself.

The Sonoran Desert

Saguaro Cactus

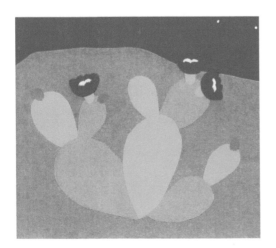

Nopales

The Sonoran Desert is a large desert that includes land in two countries, Mexico and the United States. It has more animals and plants than any other desert in the United States, some of which are found nowhere else in the world. That is because this desert is warm in the winter as well as the summer. There are 350 kinds of birds, 20 amphibians, 100 reptiles, 1000 native bees, and 2000 native plants. People live here too! Two large cities, Phoenix and Tuscon, are in this desert.

Saguaro cacti live only in the Sonoran Desert. They can live to be 200 years old and grow very slowly. A 10 year old saguaro is only 15 inches high! Saguaros can grow up to 60 feet tall which is as tall as ten people stacked up. These cactus have spines, white flowers and red fruit. Many animals visit them to find a place to live or eat a meal.

Nopales, also know as prickly pear, are in the cacti family. They live in places with mild winters, hot summers and low rainfall. They are 88% water! They have edible fruits and the paddles can be eaten if you take off the spines.

Desert pocket mice have tails almost as long as their bodies. They live in the sand dunes and shrubs in the driest parts of the Sonoran Desert. They live alone, eat seeds from plants, and don't need to drink water. They get all the water they need from the seeds they eat.

Desert
Pocket Mouse

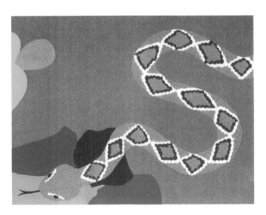

Western diamondback rattlesnakes are 4-5 feet long. At the end of their tail they have a rattle that they use to warn other animals to stay away. Their bite is poisonous, so stay away if you hear that rattle or see one! They can sense temperature which helps them to find meals. They eat small amimals like mice, birds, lizards, and rabbits. Snakes need to stay cool in the hot summer desert so they will spend all day underground or in the shade and come out when it is cooler.

Western
Diamondback
Rattlesnake

Coyotes are in the same animal family as dogs but they are wild animals. They can run up to 40 miles an hour, run on their toes, and can jump very high. They are talkative animals and you can often hear them yipping, howling, and barking at night. They form packs and live in underground dens. Coyotes are highly adaptable and live in the desert, woods, and even cities!

Western Coyote

The elf owl is the tiniest owl in the world! They have excellent eyes and ears, and silent flight. They live in the Sonoran Desert near water or near saguaro cactuses, and nest high in a cactus or tree. They hunt at night and eat mostly insects.

Elf Owl

CPSIA information can be obtained
at www.ICGtesting.com
Printed in the USA
JSHW040751120723
44438JS00001B/4